THIS BOOK WAS CREATED AS A RESULT OF YEARS STANDING BESIDE FAMILIES AS THEY EXPERIENCED THE LOSS OF A CHILD. THIS BOOK IS INTENDED TO BRING COMFORT TO THE CHILDREN THAT ARE ALSO AFFECTED. IT INCLUDES A LOT OF PRAYERS AND GOD'S GRACE.

ILLUSTRATIONS BY: BANGBARONS

WHERE DID MOMMY'S BABY GO?

BY Autumn Doan

ILLUSTRATIONS BY BANGBARONS

TAKE HEART, MY CHILD.
FOR HE HOLDS US.

CLOSELY & DEARLY.

MOMMY AND DADDY TOLD US WE WERE GOING TO HAVE ANOTHER BABY.

WE WERE VERY EXCITED!

MOMMY WENT TO THE DOCTOR TO CHECK ON THE BABY EVERY MONTH. DADDY WENT, TOO.

THE DOCTOR SAID THE BABY WAS GROWING BIG.

EXCEPT, ONE DAY BEFORE
THE BABY WAS BORN,
SOMETHING SAD HAPPENED.

DADDY SAID THE BABY
"DIDN'T MAKE IT."

I DIDN'T REALLY KNOW WHAT
THAT MEANT BUT I KNOW THAT
MOMMY AND DADDY WERE SAD.

THEY GOT TO HOLD THE BABY BUT
THE BABY COULDN'T COME HOME.

I WAS SAD, TOO.

MOMMY CRIED A LOT.

DADDY WAS SAD, TOO –
BUT HE TOOK ME OUTSIDE TO
PLAY EVERY DAY UNTIL
MOMMY STARTED TO FEEL BETTER.

IT HELPED MAKE US SMILE.

ONE DAY, MOMMY STARTED
PLAYING, TOO.

SHE SMILED AT ME.

AND HUGGED ME VERY TIGHT.

I ASKED HER WHAT HAPPENED TO THE BABY.

SHE KISSED MY HEAD AND SAID, "THE BABY WENT TO HEAVEN TO PLAY WITH JESUS AND THE OTHER BABIES THAT JUST COULDN'T COME HOME."

I LIKED IT WHEN THE FAMILY
WOULD TALK ABOUT THE BABY.

THEY SAID THE BABY'S NAME A LOT.
MOM ESPECIALLY LIKED THAT.

MOMMY AND DADDY SAID
MAYBE ONE DAY WE COULD
HAVE ANOTHER BABY.

BUT I WILL ALWAYS LOVE
THIS BABY, TOO.

Made in the USA
Las Vegas, NV
13 December 2024

14137046R00019